This Thirst

D1383924

This Thirst

Poems by

M.J. Iuppa

Kelsay Books

Cover art: © 2017 Elizabeth King Durand, *Thirst*, an intaglio monoprint with collage.

ISBN: 13-978-1-945752-96-4

Kelsay Books
Aldrich Press
www.kelsaybooks.com

For my husband Peter Tonery
& children,
George D. Marron, Meghan Rose and Nicholas P. Tonery

Acknowledgments

I am grateful to the editors of the following journals where these poems, or earlier versions, first appeared.

Allegro Poetry Magazine, Blue Heron Review, Canto Magazine, Clementine Poetry Journal, Corvus Review, Dead Snakes, Digging to the Roots Poetry Calendar 2015, Eunoia Review, Festival Writer, Flutter Journal, Fredericksburg Literary Review, Freshwater Literary Journal, Front Porch Review, H_NGM_N, Jellyfish Whispers, Kind of a Hurricane Press: Secrets & Dreams, Le Mot Juste, 2016, Poetry Pacific, Poetry Storehouse, Poppy Road Review, Silver Birch Press, Where I Live, Poetry and Photography Series, Snapdragon, A Journal of Art & Healing, Tar River Poetry, The Lake (UK), The Literary Nest, The Notebook, The Plum Tree Tavern, and When Women Waken, Being Anthology.

Contents

THREE

About the Author

ONE

What Words Would Do?

Snow blows through trembling trees
leaving nothing to immortality.
                              I'm struck
by the facets of a minute snowflake stuck
on my wool coat's lapel
                    & hold my breath
to let it last long enough to catch a pinpoint
of light before it disappears.

I Am Happy to Be Standing Here

Like a bad metaphor, I think
I know something that you
need to know. I think

it's a parable that wants
to be a conversation between
two dodgy listeners. I think

you can lose your shadow
in the river, whether it's
rushing or still.

Today, I dedicate this
to you, you who dare
to follow me.

Taking Your Time

On this dark morning in November, the candle's amber
light struggles against chill, against shadows, pooling
in corners, waiting to slither away with the hour you've
just lost to the hall clock's sweeping hands.

You can't fix this. Every year, just when you think you
have mastered the hour that puts you ahead, you find
yourself, waking to an hour that repeats itself.
It doesn't matter what happened.

Don't wish for the candle's eternal light. It has an empty
side. Holiness has time on its hands. Think of your family
as an orchard heavy with apples. You have a penknife
and a loaf of crusty bread. Think of what you can do

that *isn't* in books. You won't expire, not in this hour's
half-light. Winter is coming— time to put tired things away.

A Brief Spell

At the picture window, I sway in time with the pin oak's branches
slow lift then quick dip, seemingly caught in the excitement
of sudden wind and rain and errant flakes of snow.

Among these minutes, darkness comes, filling in the airy
spaces. No glimpse of moon or star, only the evening's
cool periwinkle.

If I were outside, this brief spell could cure loneliness.
The weather's uncertainty, its push and pull, could
be a gift of gathering, of letting go.

Good Will

1.
O empty sky, will it rain?
Sunflowers lean heavy-headed against a worn fence.
Like refugees, they wait for a message
to fall from a passing bird's beak . . .

2.
Who sent you?
Shadow, that loses its head, its hand,
pushes through the doorway—
the scent of the garden on your skin.

3.
If I turn around quickly, will I see my past?
The sound of the brass bell is gone,
and with it, cherry cobbler served in glass bowls—
my boarding pass to a cloistered life of schoolgirls.

4.
Where can you buy findings called etcetera?
Metaphors can be hooks and eyes and snaps—
a box full of lonely buttons—zippers without teeth.
Anything I wish for, found in an old dresser drawer.

Boy with Bird, 1964

after a color woodcut by Masuo Ikeda

Outside an open doorway, a boy
sits cross-legged—his silky black
hair falls over his eyes.

Evening's bronze shadows
pool around his slender body,
holding him still.

From dusty eaves, a sparrow
flutters, landing on his shoulder.
Without fear, it looks deeply

into the boy's eyes for a long
time, waiting for tears to fall
freely & quench its thirst.

Not Spring, But Nearly Spring

Despite foreclosure, so many
buds swell on apple trees
with expectation . . .

The orchard hasn't been touched
in a decade.
          Still, something stirs
within these mottled boughs—filmy
petals float on twiggy fingertips

 like faint promises.
          We forget
the apple will be many apples,
no matter what happens
in town.

Rain

Slow, at first, then over-
flowing, a flood that no one
warned us was coming from
a distance, so far away.

So Many Layers of Gray

Curse me, my thumb bleeds—silver roadside thistle, gone to needle,
pricks a warning—I didn't heed its message from death.
I didn't think of prophesy. I didn't know the rickety door
to this world would bring me maturity.

What else will be mine before sundown?
I stand toothless—my thumb soaks
in my mouth's comfort.

I think god knows how this ends—
disheveled—dragging an arm through
a discarded winter coat—I turn
blank face to the countryside burning
in autumn's fire & think I'm the window
washer's widow.

I haven't seen clearly for a year, living
in the dark city of my head.

It Was That Time of Thaw

when March kept gray rooms & windows
were veiled in winter's grime.
Our chilly farmhouse waited to tick-tick
beneath wind's backlash
& tree fingers tapped on sills.

Our children grew older & disappeared,
one by one, leaving behind bedrooms
full of thunderclouds.
We closed doors on tipped universes,
keeping what's left of wilderness
untouched.

When our cats wander up the back
stairs, I imagine them searching
for rooms full of buttery sunlight,
a mound of clothes on an unmade
bed, a perfect reason for
stepping in.

Par Avion

Over the lake this morning, clouds
appear dinghy white, like a blanket
slipping off the foot of an unmade
bed without a *shhh*—
                  Still, clouds thicken—
rolling folds drop to the horizon's
blue mail slot that's waiting for
an envelope addressed to you.

(It Doesn't Matter What Happened)

The air is fidgety inside the conversation
balloons inflating above our heads:

O, molecules, how can you be so cruel?
Snapdragons rattle on the windowsill.

We're stunned to think of what we've said
with our backs turned.

Gravity

It is windy this evening, and dark, but not cold.
The red votive lit on the windowsill sputters.
I fold laundry & hold the first shirt's warmth
to my face. I'm thinking of how many times

I have worn this shirt. It's faded into a shape
that remembers what I once was. It forgives
me each time I put it on. I'm sure Newton
omitted this law of nature. I must look it up.

To know how to fold clothes before I die.
To know I could put all the clothes away,
right away. Now that would be satisfaction.
Outside everything is moving in   & out

of sync. The wind gusts & sighs, carrying
on, carrying on . . .

Wheel of Fortune

Meaningless, at first—
spider silks balloon over-
head, in bright sun.

You don't look where
you're going, which
is more about life

than living, so
you act like every-
thing is intentional,

like this day's whirl-
pool, spinning you in
the direction of what's

waiting for you.

Gracenotes

Turning & turning, O melon
moon drop your amber light

upon the orchard that's heavy
with red fruit & waiting to be

plucked by just so many brown
hands who know how to measure

every moment for goodness' sake
in their fingertips, without bruising

flesh beneath skins—tangy sweet-
ness intact as invisible lips smack

with little kisses, not good bye
world of daylight diving back-

wards into Ontario's indigo water,
disappearing before the great

blue heron sees its chance.

One Apple Among Many

If my appetite matched my eye's desire
to smell, to bite, to taste what I've picked
loose from a branch high over my head, I

would hold its shape of plenty close
to my chest, hoping for a moment where
I am completely calm and able to carry

this apple, cradled among many, back
to the kitchen sink without letting
it fall with certain explosion

onto the orchard's eternal grasses.
If—my whole life has wagered on
the conditional tense—what would

happen if I took a bite? Would I
be closer to the man who taught me
how to dream?

Without Force

Rain came last night and I didn't hear it. Instead I listened to the box fan's purr as I slept
beneath a thin cotton sheet. I didn't dream

of sunlight in trees or red hens dusting
up a storm, or the leopard frog's stony
eyes peering out of the murky pond. I

can't say how I woke up in the same
position, at the hour I fell asleep, only
it's a different day and it rained with-

out a sound, giving morning its first
breath in a hundred days of holding. I
too can't ignore this washed air, this

bead of water caught in an oak leaf,
finding its release, quick
& silent.

TWO

Resistance

Beyond a rain-speckled window, fog
rises in the orchard.
                    Drifting green mist
insinuates a temporary peace, passing
its light tulle over what can't be lifted
into the sky.
A book slides off my lap, opening
to a photograph of resistance:
A lone man walking the middle of the road,
stands directly in front of a line
of Chinese tanks that have been summed
to Tiananmen. He is diverting tension,
weaving side to side, climbing the face
of the tank's artillery in his attempt
to get inside . . . He is lost to history.
No one knows where he is, but always
he is here . . .
Radio says to expect more rain.
Another night without seeing the stars
punctuating the endless sky, I think I
can keep my mind quiet enough
to see something I believed was lost.

Ontario Chronicle, 1970

I was the one who waited on the battered dock
until the last possible moment, hypnotized
by the sun's blood-orange tokens dimpling
the lake's slow swell of waves rising but
not breaking before reaching the lee shore.
I remember dreaming then, my future sealed
in the horizon's thin envelope of light.

Where did it go?
                        Love called me to hurry
back to the bonfires burning bright—the bird-
house with its nesting purple martins—some
flew beyond the drizzle of sparks to feed on
mosquitoes stirred up by billowing smoke.

Tourists found this summer ritual a prophesy:
the fierce chrysanthemum arcing in the night
sky—iridescent petals floating on Ontario's
stillness. I found this summons to walk
its shimmering path
terrifying—

We Stopped at Onondaga Lake
before Coming Home

Remembering his words, like eating a sweet haven
peach, and not being prepared for the juice to burst
in its ripeness, dripping everywhere, and so sticky
that it was hard to wipe it up, even the smell
lingered for most of the day—that one complete
smell that was him and his words, the way he said
he wanted to love me for a long time, for a very long
time—I still regret I was there, sitting next to him
on the riprap surrounding a dead lake, listening
to cicadas simmer high in the crowns of black willows,
watching a strider streak across the water's glassy
surface—feeling a disturbance in my universe.

How Do You Stop Her?

Bird fidget—bony hand splayed open then closed, thumb
curved in a lie: *how do you stop her?*

She pretends to know a great deal when she sees it:
the box of loose baby doll parts found in Goodwill.

Stuck eyes, smudged porcelain heads, matted hair, limbs
akimbo, such a shame.

A puzzle that's out of place, finds a place on her shelf.
She's sorting it out on Instagram.

Ne'er do well friends send her cryptic notes that she
reads with her lips to a cold glass chardonnay.

You're not touching this baby, she twitters.

Standing on Top of a Skyscraper about to Scream

I lost an earring today. My signature
style, a gift 2555 days ago, and now I
have one moon, one star, one sun
instead of two.
                    Where is it? Stuck in
a crack somewhere? I can't imagine re-
tracing steps back to the moment it
slipped off nonchalantly, without me
feeling it until I felt it—my fingers
pinching my earlobes as if it just
happened—my scarf the culprit.

Below I see traffic stop & go,
its music strikes a chord that I
can't match. Somewhere down
there, on the avenue's sidewalk
my earring's sun and moon and star
lies crumpled up, waiting for the stranger
who wears one earring to pick it up . . .

Why We Didn't Have More Time Together

When death is no longer mysterious, when we realize
it's a one way ticket heading west to a destination
that will be free of forethought, then we'll find our-

selves ready to lie down on a grassy bank to watch
the creek's still water, the cinnamon ant balancing
on the tip of a blade of grass, reaching with delight.

It's a sermon we rarely hear, but in spring, it sounds
like sun & wind, recalling relationships forgotten
in winter. Listen closely, we have put off too many

things—our minds, full of messages not sent because
we're too busy doing as we please, which is more
puzzling than death, don't you think?

Last Intention

Daybreak, and the blown leaf pressed against the window
could be an angel's dusty wing or a lost brown bird. I'm
not sure what has been thrown off course in this season
between seasons; still not Spring, something is stubborn
in this weather's map, swirling with so many delays.
What do I know? I'm not sure if the good-natured part
of love is waiting. But I am.

With(out)

Standing on the pier, beneath restless clouds
without an umbrella, I watch a slow curtain of
rain sweep across the horizon—its dark blue
hem dragging against the swell of white capped
waves heading towards shore.

Soon, rain will surround me, and I will be
soaked in that old & empty odor that tastes
oddly metallic yet certainly bitter as autumn's
worn vocabulary. All my life I have wanted
to watch without being touched.

As if living could be seen behind glass, like
a miniature Victorian Village. I wanted a life
where I was left alone, not out of selfishness
or forgetfulness— no, no, not that at all. Still this

want comes & goes like these white capped waves
rising, rising to fall flat faced against the pier's
concrete, against me with a force that anoints me,
face first, without protection.

How Much Did Brahms Know about
Pulling Strings?

Is it safe to sit in the intimacy of chamber music,
when your spirits sink in the thoughts of what's
waiting for you?

Your hands are empty. No longer safe, gripping
a pen's fine point, writing glossy notes to those
who will never listen to your advisement, but
rush to the inked grade that awaits them.

Judgment, you think, is negligible. You listen
to the violin's insistent question to the cello's
constant measure & wonder if it's unimportant—
who's listening really?

Like Brahms, what you love has made
a fool of you.

Before Darkness Comes

After a day of rain, of sleep-walking room
to room, wondering what else can be made
with the last peck of pickles, twilight arrives

candling the sky with streaks of indigo
and deep pink—an invitation to step
outside before it's too late . . .

Who can resist distraction?

And so we go to the lake to walk
along its rain-dimpled beach that holds
Ontario's stillness within its margins.

Only intermittent drips of rain falling
from the canopy of silver beech leaves
disturb this quiet, enough to make us look

up and beyond our stopping—the slightest
slip of wave rinses over a cache of cobbles
unearthed in the storm—to relish all

that waits patiently to be noticed before
darkness comes.

Everyday Eccentrics

Restless air stirs our atmosphere, inside and out—clouds of fruit flies grow
thinner in the steady steam of putting
by as glass jars line up like an infantry
on the dining room table, ready
to be marched to the root cellar's hold
to keep us through another winter.

But, for now, we count what we have:
the sweet fire of tomato sauce glowing
in morning's light, the jams of a hundred
days of summer; the stewed, the pickled,
the sundried—secret recipes that invite
us to supper with the past that's not
vague or shiftless. We know what
we've made makes you curious
to taste the difference.

This Thirst

There is a long thirst that comes in the hours
past midnight. It wakes me from my nightly
dream of climbing a rough-faced mountain.

This thirst pulls me up out of bed without
waking you, and before my eyes can see, I
find myself in the amber hue of the night-

light where I steady myself against the cool
bath basin . . . . Before I reach to draw water, I
spot a tent moth, that has found its way to love

the warm light, resting with its mouth
pressed against the drain, drinking deeply
the drip of water that pools there.

I have an impulse to touch its owl-like
wings to see if it's still alive, but hesitate
when I see my brute hand reaching down,

knowing that both of us have surrendered
to this moment, and neither one of us
have grasped our dream.

The Berries and The Tree

1.
As quiet light settles on the mulberry tree,
a slow current of air hushes its glossy leaves;
careful not to rouse intoxicated robins asleep
in its high crown.

2.
Happened before—sudden rain of ripe red berries
splattering the ground in the ruckus of wings ascending—
the sound, a summons to the chickens' delight
finding this good fortune ahead of the fox.

3.
Or you, curious to taste this berry's appeal, holding
one thoughtfully on your tongue—letting it melt
down to kindness—allows you to cherish
what becomes your acquired taste.

Bird, Fish

Standing at the pond's edge, silence
hooks me. I always think of us
by water, sitting on riprap
sharing what we have
with each other.

We fish the pond's reflection,
weaving one dream into another—
a strider's quick emotion stirs
our ecology and we stare
& stare into its chilly hour . . .

I think of our past, living here
where fog rises in whispers
& the flight of figures streaks
across evening's pale sky.
Soon, we will wade into another

life—one I won't be able to interrupt—
although you know I'll try
to reach you, wherever
your thoughts are
will be enough.

Capsized

Beneath a black willow, a wooden boat
stuck in sand & snake grass appears

broken by years of work on water
that trembled with weather, ripe

& ready to diminish any net's haul,
leaving you with rain in your ears—

marking the place where you stopped
irrevocably to listen to wind's consuming

laughter that soon became your tears.

Warning Signs

Once again, autumn has come around with
its precision of sun, rain, wind, shuffling
colors: buttery yellow, mallow, shell-shocked
red in the woods that rarely suppresses itself.

We walk a straight line, following a jittery
light on the ground that's covered in haircap
moss, to the banks of Howden pond where
we stand with our hands in our pockets

& take in what we cannot touch: clusters
of asters, dizzy with bees' final work—
dangerous clouds held captive in the pond's
green eye—aspen leaves shuddering in
a sudden gust of air.

Once again, we're made thoughtful.
We see that we're about to lose everything to this season that gives, and gives
and takes quickly, away.

Parable of the Cricket

It's risky letting me into your farmhouse.
One of me will wreck your solitude.

I am troubadour, dressed in black
for an evening's concert

that never-ends
like rain or promise

of windfall, you wonder
how such a big voice turns up

beneath the woodstove?
You listen to my dusky song

with your cup of tea
as if it's just another season.

Do not attempt to usher me out
unless you hear nothing.

THREE

Another Selfie

What woke me this morning wasn't the robin in
the crabapple, its insistent summons of *sweet-sweet-low,*
or the steamy gush of the coffee dripping to its brim,
or the phone's set ring tone of Custer's cavalry
charge; and it certainly wasn't my mother singing, *rise
and shine, rise and shine,* with a side of bacon
and brown toast—no, no, that wasn't what woke me;
it was the eerie silence in our bedroom, the absence of
you fast asleep next to me—my groggy eyes trying
to shake the sleep that eluded me for most of the night
as I felt your side of the bed and found that it was cold, so
utterly cold, that I knew it was time to get up.

Night of the Full Moon

What is calm in unmown grass?
Is it the lack of winter that swirls
swatches of tourmaline, cresting
like waves?

Moonlight everywhere—rust-scented
shadows dragging their weight across
the yard without a groan—nothing
disturbs the sleep of ducks.

Nothing vanishes in silence between steps,
between heartbeats . . . The break in the air's
slight movement is a gesture to settle down . . .
and something does resolve in moonlight's

lack of hurry—an hour erasing the shadow
that stops me without consequence of
weather—a door left half-closed
behind me.

For a Split Second

When the night's quiet fits snugly in your ears
& air hisses like the recorded gap before music
begins, you have an uncanny suspicion that
the quickening beat of blood pulsating is
a sound you have learned to ignore, like
the tick of a clock, or the cat's purr, or a child
dreaming—and for a split second, your ears
chime in—each tick, click, um of tongue or
breath becomes as fresh as honeysuckle or
 murmur of bees hidden in blossoms, or flash
of goldfish in the pond that has survived
another generation, in spite of being taken
for granted these many years . . .
                Only now, you want to talk
to your mother about what you've learned
without her fear of losing something—
                What was it, exactly?
You shake your head, like a sealed jar, to see
if your ears are ready to be opened.

Proverb

What day is today?
Pickling jars brought up from the cellar, gleam
on the counter, full of the tang of summer; and outside
the dill's head doesn't rattle but winnows snow until
it becomes a pinwheel, a star.

Today needs direction.
Wind has greased the weathervane
to spin without sound; and it rains then snows.
Lie down. Today is yours.

Seeing Mountains

in shades of amber, an ecology of ash
& aspens, their expansive reach to a cloud
chasing sky casts a spell over me . . .

I look up into heights I rarely perceive
from a farm whose land was once smoothed
by the press of a glacier's hand.

                                And so, I slide
into the pool of my shadow & sit there quietly
waiting for the windless explosion of monarch

wings or a thousand leaves tumbling like loose
coins tossed into autumn's sunlight to take
my breath away.

Roots and All

Tuft of celery pulled, roots and all, in my hand, I
hold its scent of water under morning's first light,
and think nothing is as clean as this is, roots and all,
a season called easy breath & downy flake, I think
I've missed its subtle kiss in my distraction, stopping
by woods full of rain & slippery squat stones that
cross a sandy creek as it merely rolls away—all in all,
I have been brought to my senses, knowing this is nothing
less than celery, which can start over, and I do, saving
it on the kitchen sill in a small jam jar, roots and all.

The Uncertainty of Winter

No snow blooms on hedges
Everywhere is green—sudden
rash of magnolia buds, tipped
silver, candles morning's light
Beauty, briefly spent

Salvation

It is cold this morning. My body's spontaneous shiver
shakes off the dampness that seeps & seeps & seeps
into every weakness, visible and invisible, making it
difficult to think of anything other than cold—everything has stopped short, yet feels like eternity. I don't
want this to be my last thought, like my tongue's memory
stuck to the icy black lamppost that was tasted on a dare
while we waited impatiently in the cold to be picked up
from the convent's curb. This morning I want to fly—arms
outstretched—as I did as a child, waiting for a quick
dismissal from the cold with a simple prayer: *O sweet jesus,
take me in your heart for a while.*

Delta

See how steady a drizzle of snow falls
when there is no wind.

O, quiet industry of weather,
here pyramids are built in a day.

Under a watermarked sky,
they rise within the space of breath.

Beyond—
in Ontario's slow swells, loons

dive—resurface,
                    float—

between forever and now.
I walk an icy path, hesitating—

if I knew what happens next,
I could give up.

Deep Cold of Winter

Is there a chance I will get a clear look at these woods?
Framed in our picture window, trees huddle close together,
a tight space I've drawn in pen & ink, in watery blues,

struggling not to spoil the light snow falling like moths
caught in a mason jar—the muffled coo of mourning
doves roosting on silvery branches . . . I think the deep

cold will seize my breath if I were to go out there
and stand with my hands in my pockets & wait
for the solitary moment to make sense, in the way black

& white makes sense in winter, where the out-of-the-blue
trill of a cardinal's dusky notes sounds flawless—a song
sung with a splash of red . . . I know the canvas of

words has so many possibilities like my paintings
made from something real & unpredictable as living
here without a lasting outline.

Dead Pine

Late afternoon in mid-winter in
a stand of trees, steel gray shadows
streak across untouched snow.

Above, steadfast skies remain
clear and blue—as the echo
of slow melting snow—

as the ache of trees swaying
to touch each other slightly
becomes visible to the one

who is dying without miracle—
the wither that vanishes
like forgetting.

Let This Be Enough

Brooklyn, 2014

Walking in Prospect Park, on Christmas Eve, I
can't help but think of my sneakers fitting inside
footprints of all sizes that wore down this hard-
parked earth, these streets, & stairways with
the weight of life's intangible desires, that no
doubt spurred them on in blind faith. I believe
this is why I'm lagging in this walk around
the park's circumference, watching the strides
of everyone who fail to match mine; even the old
terrier, who drags his leash to the curb, lifts his
wet nose to sniff the hint of Spring, like the confused
clump of snowdrops in full bloom among curled oak
leaves & ivy . . . I think I'm spoiled given this
opportunity to see people & places change
ever-so-slightly—grasping what's obvious
to a stranger, who has never lived anywhere.

Something, which is

I am not like the sycamore, willing
to disrobe in the dead of winter.
My mottled skin shields me from
the streetlight's dreary buzz.

I am out of practice, like
the sky's inability to shake snow
from its sleeves; yet, my footsteps
disappear in thin air—

I am set loose upon the world.
To go the right way would take
advantage of happiness. *And why not?*
This quirky thought, without design.

Forethought

Once manicured, now fallow
this winter field is left alone
with the stubble of its past.

A solitary crow floats over-
head, coasting on wind's
short-sightedness.

Nature can only do so
much. I hear my heart-
beat when I least expect

it, reminding me that I
have grown accustomed
to this stillness.

The barn's gutter leaks snow-
melt that will rust the gate's
hinge. I gather my strength

for another day, knowing I
will have to pry my way
back into the field.

Belongings

Lingering near a window's tense twilight,
I want to welcome winter's first snow
without dread. Its chill and light dust

makes me think of housekeeping,
the way I push things around day to
day, saving stuff that's seemingly

weightless—floating stacks of paper,
of books, of letters that matter in the ways
knowing a second language matters.

I want transparency that slides side-
ways, like a skin of ice on the cat's
water dish left on the porch.

To see what's beneath the surface:
A little madness, a little grief,
a strange collection of no two things

alike—I want to store that in
my house of footnotes when I can
no longer see the snow-covered road.

Reprieve

A stone, a feather, a shell—Ontario's
winter shoreline, windswept steps fade
away in a stretch of blue sand where a smoky
horizon smudges a temporal seal of sky
& water—its subconscious, rising
like cold moonlight on a path that tilts
in & out of fog—a paradise few find
at a glance, but those who do, disappear
in its obscurity, leaving behind
a stone, a feather, a shell.

Hereafter

In defiance of snow, she puts her shovel away in
the recesses of her old barn, behind boxes of stuff
collected over years of wishful thinking, the odds
'n ends of invention left with unread instruction
manuals that would tell her how to use her time
wisely. She hides the shovel next to elaborate
cobwebs that appear gray and filmy, dripping
like wisteria blossoms . . .
She looks all around and realizes that too many
things have complicated her life. However, snow
will no longer be one of them.

Hard to Forget What the Heart Asks

Years ago, I was slight enough to slip between raindrops.

Without intention, I worn black Chinese slippers; floated
on light kisses, on steps I wouldn't dream of taking now.

There were doors that opened & closed without a sound.

I slept on blanket hand-me-downs, among hardcover books
open to passages I would learn by the blush of dawn.

Sleep rarely came with dreams; yet, when I awoke, I found
words ink-stained on my palms. I drew figures, women

in repose. I remember thinking that it took such steady
work to be idle.

Like saved postage stamps, it would cost me my life.

About the Author

M.J. Iuppa is the Director of the Visual and Performing Arts Minor Program, Writer-in-Residence (1999-2015) and Lecturer in Creative Writing at St. John Fisher College; and since 2000 to present, is a part time lecturer in Creative Writing at The College at Brockport. Since 1986, she has been a teaching artist, working with students, K-12, in Rochester, NY, and surrounding area. She has three full length poetry collections, most recently *Small Worlds Floating* (2016) as well as *Within Reach* (2010) both from Cherry Grove Collections; *Night Traveler* (Foothills Publishing, 2003); and 5 chapbooks, most recent is *Between Worlds* (Foothills Publishing, 2013), which is a collection of lyric essays, flash fiction and prose poems. She received Writers and Books' The Big Pencil Award, honoring her lifelong contributions to Rochester's Literary Community. At St. John Fisher College, she has received the Part-Time Faculty Award for Teaching Excellence, May 2000; The Father Dorsey Award, 2000-2001 and 2002-2003, and a Certification of Recognition from The Monroe County Legislature, April 2003. Most recently awarded the New York State Chancellor's Award for Excellence in Adjunct Teaching, 2017. She served as the poetry advisor for New York State Foundation for the Arts, 2007-2012. She and her husband Peter Tonery lives on a small farm in Hamlin NY, where they have been practicing organic food sustainability for the past 16 years.